My tasks

My ideas

My goals

Grateful success
by effectively writing!

kosmidis.ch

Imprint

© 2016 Athos Kosmidis

ISBN-13: 978-1-5236-52-77-8

More about the author can be found at www.kosmidis.ch

Cover design: Zeljka Kojic / Athos Kosmidis

Printed by CreateSpace, An Amazon.com Company

Bibliographic information of the German National Library

The German National Library lists this publication in the German National; detailed bibliographic data is available on the Internet at http://dnb.d-nb.de.

This book belongs to

_____

_____

E-Mail

_____

_____

Phone

_____

_____

Grateful success
by effectively writing!

It usually Takes 72 Hours!

If you want to implement a new idea successfully, make sure that the first 72 hours (3 days!) are decisive. Organize your projects and start with the implementation. Make sure to schedule and prioritize!

Resist the beginnings!

The first day of your working week is the most important.

- Set deadlines

- Do important tasks!

Everything you need to tackle the week is on the first working day will attract positive and grateful success by itself. - The rest of the week will be a breeze!

Grateful success by effectively writing!

Here we go!

I hope you enjoy,

and good luck!

I wish you success as you
plan your tasks and
successfully solve them.

Grateful success
by effectively writing!

Grateful success
by effectively writing!

Write down here your…	○
tasks ideas objectives	✓
	○
	○
	○
	○
	○
	○
	○
	○
	○
	○
	○
	○
	○
	○

Grateful success
by effectively writing!

Grateful success
by effectively writing!

Write down here your...	○
tasks ideas objectives	✓
	○
	○
	○
	○
	○
	○
	○
	○
	○
	○
	○
	○
	○
	○

Grateful success
by effectively writing!

Write down here your...	○
tasks ideas objectives	✓
	○
	○
	○
	○
	○
	○
	○
	○
	○
	○
	○
	○
	○
	○
	○

Grateful success by effectively writing!

Write down here your...	○
tasks ideas objectives	✓
	○
	○
	○
	○
	○
	○
	○
	○
	○
	○
	○
	○
	○
	○

Grateful success
by effectively writing!

Grateful success
by effectively writing!

Write down here your...	○
tasks ideas objectives	✓
	○
	○
	○
	○
	○
	○
	○
	○
	○
	○
	○
	○
	○
	○

Grateful success
by effectively writing!

Grateful success
by effectively writing!

Write down here your...	○
tasks ideas objectives	✓
	○
	○
	○
	○
	○
	○
	○
	○
	○
	○
	○
	○
	○
	○
	○

Grateful success
by effectively writing!

Grateful success
by effectively writing!

Write down here your…	○
tasks ideas objectives	✓
	○
	○
	○
	○
	○
	○
	○
	○
	○
	○
	○
	○
	○

Grateful success
by effectively writing!

Write down here your...	○
tasks ideas objectives	✓
	○
	○
	○
	○
	○
	○
	○
	○
	○
	○
	○
	○
	○
	○
	○

*Grateful success
by effectively writing!*

Grateful success
by effectively writing!

Write down here your...	○
tasks ideas objectives	✓
	○
	○
	○
	○
	○
	○
	○
	○
	○
	○
	○
	○
	○
	○

Grateful success
by effectively writing!

Write down here your…	○
tasks ideas objectives	✓
	○
	○
	○
	○
	○
	○
	○
	○
	○
	○
	○
	○
	○
	○
	○
	○

Grateful success
by effectively writing!

Write down here your...	◯
tasks ideas objectives	✓
	◯
	◯
	◯
	◯
	◯
	◯
	◯
	◯
	◯
	◯
	◯
	◯
	◯
	◯
	◯

Grateful success
by effectively writing!

Grateful success
by effectively writing!

Write down here your...

tasks   ideas   objectives ✓

Grateful success
by effectively writing!

Grateful success
by effectively writing!

Write down here your…	○
tasks ideas objectives	✓
	○
	○
	○
	○
	○
	○
	○
	○
	○
	○
	○
	○
	○
	○

Grateful success
by effectively writing!

Write down here your...	○
tasks ideas objectives	✓
	○
	○
	○
	○
	○
	○
	○
	○
	○
	○
	○
	○
	○
	○
	○

Grateful success
by effectively writing!

Grateful success
by effectively writing!

Write down here your...	○
tasks ideas objectives	✓
	○
	○
	○
	○
	○
	○
	○
	○
	○
	○
	○
	○
	○
	○

Write down here your...

tasks   ideas   objectives   ✓

Grateful success
by effectively writing!

Write down here your…	○
tasks ideas objectives	✓
	○
	○
	○
	○
	○
	○
	○
	○
	○
	○
	○
	○
	○
	○
	○

Grateful success
by effectively writing!

Write down here your...	○
tasks ideas objectives	✓
	○
	○
	○
	○
	○
	○
	○
	○
	○
	○
	○
	○
	○
	○

Grateful success
by effectively writing!

Grateful success
by effectively writing!

Write down here your...	○
tasks ideas objectives	✓
	○
	○
	○
	○
	○
	○
	○
	○
	○
	○
	○
	○
	○
	○

Grateful success
by effectively writing!

Grateful success
by effectively writing!

Write down here your…	○
tasks ideas objectives	✓
	○
	○
	○
	○
	○
	○
	○
	○
	○
	○
	○
	○
	○
	○

Grateful success
by effectively writing!

Grateful success
by effectively writing!

Write down here your...	○
tasks ideas objectives	✓
	○
	○
	○
	○
	○
	○
	○
	○
	○
	○
	○
	○
	○
	○

Grateful success
by effectively writing!

Grateful success
by effectively writing!

Write down here your...	○
tasks ideas objectives	✓
	○
	○
	○
	○
	○
	○
	○
	○
	○
	○
	○
	○
	○
	○

*Grateful success
by effectively writing!*

Write down here your...	○
tasks ideas objectives	✓
	○
	○
	○
	○
	○
	○
	○
	○
	○
	○
	○
	○
	○
	○

Grateful success
by effectively writing!

Grateful success
by effectively writing!

Write down here your...	○
tasks ideas objectives	✓
	○
	○
	○
	○
	○
	○
	○
	○
	○
	○
	○
	○
	○
	○
	○

Grateful success
by effectively writing!

Write down here your...

tasks   ideas   objectives   ✓

Grateful success
by effectively writing!

Write down here your...	○
tasks ideas objectives	✓
	○
	○
	○
	○
	○
	○
	○
	○
	○
	○
	○
	○
	○
	○

Grateful success
by effectively writing!

Grateful success
by effectively writing!

Write down here your...	○
tasks ideas objectives	✓
	○
	○
	○
	○
	○
	○
	○
	○
	○
	○
	○
	○
	○
	○
	○

Grateful success
by effectively writing!

Write down here your...	○
tasks ideas objectives	✓
	○
	○
	○
	○
	○
	○
	○
	○
	○
	○
	○
	○
	○
	○

Grateful success
by effectively writing!

Write down here your…	○
tasks ideas objectives	✓
	○
	○
	○
	○
	○
	○
	○
	○
	○
	○
	○
	○
	○
	○

Grateful success
by effectively writing!

Write down here your...	○
tasks ideas objectives	✓
	○
	○
	○
	○
	○
	○
	○
	○
	○
	○
	○
	○
	○
	○

Grateful success
by effectively writing!

Write down here your…	○
tasks ideas objectives	✓
	○
	○
	○
	○
	○
	○
	○
	○
	○
	○
	○
	○
	○
	○

Write down here your... ○

tasks   ideas   objectives ✓

○

○

○

○

○

○

○

○

○

○

○

○

○

○

○

Grateful success
by effectively writing!

Grateful success
by effectively writing!

Write down here your...	○
tasks ideas objectives	✓
	○
	○
	○
	○
	○
	○
	○
	○
	○
	○
	○
	○
	○
	○

Grateful success
by effectively writing!

Grateful success
by effectively writing!

Write down here your... ◯

tasks   ideas   objectives ✓

◯

◯

◯

◯

◯

◯

◯

◯

◯

◯

◯

◯

◯

Grateful success
by effectively writing!

Grateful success
by effectively writing!

Write down here your...	○
tasks ideas objectives	✓
	○
	○
	○
	○
	○
	○
	○
	○
	○
	○
	○
	○
	○
	○

Grateful success
by effectively writing!

Write down here your…	○
tasks ideas objectives	✓
	○
	○
	○
	○
	○
	○
	○
	○
	○
	○
	○
	○
	○
	○
	○

Grateful success
by effectively writing!

Write down here your...	○
tasks ideas objectives	✓
	○
	○
	○
	○
	○
	○
	○
	○
	○
	○
	○
	○
	○
	○

Grateful success
by effectively writing!

Grateful success
by effectively writing!

Write down here your...	◯
tasks ideas objectives	✓
	◯
	◯
	◯
	◯
	◯
	◯
	◯
	◯
	◯
	◯
	◯
	◯
	◯
	◯

Grateful success
by effectively writing!

Grateful success
by effectively writing!

Write down here your…	○
tasks ideas objectives	✓
	○
	○
	○
	○
	○
	○
	○
	○
	○
	○
	○
	○
	○

Grateful success
by effectively writing!

Grateful success
by effectively writing!

Write down here your...	○
tasks ideas objectives	✓
	○
	○
	○
	○
	○
	○
	○
	○
	○
	○
	○
	○
	○
	○

Grateful success
by effectively writing!

Write down here your...	○
tasks ideas objectives	✓
	○
	○
	○
	○
	○
	○
	○
	○
	○
	○
	○
	○
	○
	○
	○

Grateful success
by effectively writing!

Grateful success
by effectively writing!

Write down here your…	○
tasks ideas objectives	✓
	○
	○
	○
	○
	○
	○
	○
	○
	○
	○
	○
	○
	○
	○

Grateful success
by effectively writing!

Grateful success
by effectively writing!

Write down here your...	○
tasks ideas objectives	✓
	○
	○
	○
	○
	○
	○
	○
	○
	○
	○
	○
	○
	○
	○

*Grateful success
by effectively writing!*

Grateful success
by effectively writing!

Write down here your...

tasks   ideas   objectives   ✓

○

○

○

○

○

○

○

○

○

○

○

○

○

○

○

Grateful success
by effectively writing!

Grateful success
by effectively writing!

Write down here your…	○
tasks ideas objectives	✓
	○
	○
	○
	○
	○
	○
	○
	○
	○
	○
	○
	○
	○
	○

Grateful success
by effectively writing!

Grateful success
by effectively writing!

Write down here your...	○
tasks ideas objectives	✓
	○
	○
	○
	○
	○
	○
	○
	○
	○
	○
	○
	○
	○
	○

Grateful success
by effectively writing!

Congratulations!

To continue to successfully plan, order the next book today!

Thanks in advance!

Athos Kosmidis

Grateful success by effectively writing!

Grateful success
by effectively writing!

Write down here your...	○
tasks ideas objectives	✓
	○
	○
	○
	○
	○
	○
	○
	○
	○
	○
	○
	○
	○
	○

Grateful success
by effectively writing!

Grateful success
by effectively writing!

Write down here your…	○
tasks ideas objectives	✓
	○
	○
	○
	○
	○
	○
	○
	○
	○
	○
	○
	○
	○
	○

Grateful success
by effectively writing!

Grateful success
by effectively writing!

Write down here your…	○
tasks ideas objectives	✓
	○
	○
	○
	○
	○
	○
	○
	○
	○
	○
	○
	○
	○
	○
	○

Grateful success
by effectively writing!

Grateful success
by effectively writing!

Write down here your... ○

tasks   ideas   objectives ✓

○

○

○

○

○

○

○

○

○

○

○

○

○

○

Grateful success
by effectively writing!

"Recognize yourself!

... And only

recognize you and you understand

the relationships

in your life!"

www.kosmidis.ch